ALL THINGS TIRE OF THEMSELVES

ALL THINGS TIRE OF THEMSELVES

Poems by
Arnold Wesker

Foreword by Michael Kustow

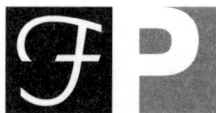

𝓕P

𝓕lambardPress

First published in Great Britain in 2008 by Flambard Press
Stable Cottage, East Fourstones, Hexham NE47 5DX
www.flambardpress.co.uk

Typeset by BookType
Cover design by Gainford Design Associates
Author photograph by John Downing, 1997
Printed in Great Britain by Cromwell Press, Trowbridge, Wiltshire

A CIP catalogue record for this book
is available from the British Library.
ISBN 978-1-873226-98-8

Flambard Press wishes to thank Arts Council England
for its financial support.

ARTS COUNCIL
ENGLAND

Flambard Press is a member of Inpress,
and of Independent Northern Publishers.

FSC   **Mixed Sources**
Product group from well-managed
forests and other controlled sources
www.fsc.org Cert no. TT-COC-2082
© 1996 Forest Stewardship Council

To my great-grandchildren
Jerome and Shadae
and to all my great-grandchildren to come
I dedicate this collection
hoping it leads them
to the pleasures of poetry

Acknowledgements

Some of the poems in this collection have been published in the following magazines, journals and anthologies: *Caravan, Contrasts, Imagen, The Jewish Chronicle, The Jewish Quarterly, Jewish Renaissance, Lebanon/Lebanon, Nineties Poetry, Occasional Poets, Overland, Piano, the sixties, Sunday Citizen, Terra Del Fucco, Write Thru The Year.*

Contents

FIVE POEMS FOR HAROLD PINTER

'STORMS' AND OTHER POEMS

LONGER POEMS

Within This Bony Barrel:
The Poems of Arnold Wesker

A Foreword by Michael Kustow

And yet within this bony barrel
Beats youth's dream.
'Old Boats'

This collection of poems – Wesker's first, culled from a lifetime of 'off-stage' writing – is a porthole into the writer's heart, an archetypal male story, the logbook of a journey as poignant as a Schubert *lied*, an extended soliloquy about family, love, ageing, anger, Jewishness.

The predominant tone is one of sadness and disenchantment, but never resignation. 'All Things Tire of Themselves', says the poet, but the life cycle is tirelessly renewed; there is a new child, a change of heart, a fresh season.

In this cluster of poems there is a drama: the struggle not to succumb to weariness of spirit in the face of the thousand natural shocks that flesh is heir to. Out of this struggle with despair, the poet delivers a hard-won wisdom, a precarious triumph over thieving time. Wesker might have chosen an epigraph for these poems from Ecclesiastes: 'To everything there is a season, and a time for every purpose under heaven.'

Twenty-five years ago, on 15 September 1982 to be exact, Wesker sent me a letter with a poem, 'which I wrote God knows why for God knows whom'. Although he hasn't included it in this book, it conjures up the same picture of a bare ending as many poems in the book express:

I have this fear of ageing maudlin
Regretting all
Pleading with my eyes and sighs
Forgiveness, sympathy
A worldly understanding
For the frailty of flesh
The collapse of passion
The intellect's senility
I have this fear.

I fear dismissal from my children
A wife's weary patience
The look in friends' eyes
Remembering, remembering
The energy, the courage
The vivid eagerness
And appetites which were
Once were.
I have this fear.

I have this fear of fading
In grey foolishness
Damp lids, weak smiles
Pubescent humour, stained trousers
And oh so very infantile
Second childhood
While I weep at nights
For the long lost first.
I have this fear.

Did I really never think I'd become
As all old men
Wretched with remorse
Frayed with guilts
Defeated by that cycle
Told from the very first of the Bible's pages
Of man's brutality
His reachings, lapsings
Futile fights against his beast?
Did I really never think my beast
Would batter beat me in the end?
I have this fear.

In the letter accompanying this untitled poem, however, Wesker hastens to add that his mood in real life is not as morose as this. '[I] can hear you sigh, "Oh Christ!" when you read it. But I don't feel as bad as this poem does. I'm relaxed and productive and reading and writing about why I'm Jewish. Did you know that I've been invited by the Rockefeller Foundation to meet with 25 other "eminent writers and literary scholars from the United States, Italy, France, England, Israel, Poland and the Soviet Union" . . . I have been invited to deliver a paper on "the survival and transformation of Jewish cultural and religious values in literature written since World War Two." So I'm reading the Bible! (Hence the line in the poem.)'

This comment is a reminder that these poems of melancholy and regret exist one step away from real life. They aren't a case-study, a literal account; they're literary enlargements. They ache, and this ache is a truth. But the real-life Wesker refuses to give way, making himself too busy to lament. His resilience is like that of many characters in his plays – like Beatie Bryant in *Roots*. The story told by both the plays and the poems is a story of defeat, but it ends in renewed striving, even exhilaration. They are a kind of heart-scan of the inner life. But though the writer's heart is bruised, it is not crushed. It has the strength to go on beating, articulating the defeats, not being buried by them.

Yet their titles are a litany of time's usury and life's losses: 'Old men cry out', 'The stumbling age', 'If we parted', 'Insomnia', 'Vain image', 'Mistakes writ large'. They make up an album of regret and grieving. Their diction, at times wilfully archaic, reminds me of the plangency of Tennyson's mourning in *In Memoriam* and of Thomas Hardy in his ballad-like poems. Wesker's emotions are often Hardy-esque, and in the most successful poems as stoic as Philip Larkin's:

> All things tire of themselves
> Be comforted be glad
> Not only the singer's joy
> But the demagogue's tongue
> The revolutionary's fervour
> All that makes love sad
> And passion
> Be comforted be glad.

The play of his which these poems most recall is *The Four Seasons*, a cyclical account of a love affair that ends elegiacally. The two one-time lovers meet again in the desolation of winter, and tell each other about who they have loved since:

ADAM. Your lover, tell me, what do you remember most about him?
BEATRICE. What do I remember? A long drive into the autumn countryside I remember. The astonish-ment we shared that trees and fields could burn with such colours. The tremendous blaze of dying hedges, the smouldering leaves. The discovery of these things. And you? What do you remember about her?
ADAM. Moments of music, silence, adoration. I remember the scrupulous care she gave to everything

12

she did for me – wrapping a present, cooking a meal, the attention of her eyes. And I remember cruelty – her cruelty and my cruelty.

BEATRICE. I remember our plots against indifference, the easy way we picked up each other's thoughts in our 'battles with the world', the language we gave each other, my gratitude for his presence, my helplessness.

ADAM. I remember that we weren't afraid to dance when we couldn't, to say we didn't know things we should have known, admit wrongs against the other.

BEATRICE. I remember that we weren't afraid to laugh hysterically or play with children or grow old. I remember we just weren't afraid. And I remember when my father died in a far-off country I didn't go to his side because I wanted to stay with my lover. My father died alone. I was his favourite child.

ADAM. And I remember my father dying and my holding his head in my hands and crying: 'Keep breathing, Joe, come on, don't give up, don't stop, Joe.' And my mother through her tears saying, 'You think he'll listen to you?' and smiling, and both of us sobbing and smiling.

They exchange smiles.

BEATRICE. Why do we remember these things I wonder?

ADAM. Oh, I don't know. Perhaps because such moments remind us time passes, and time passing reminds us of sadness, waste, neglect, suffering . . . all those lovely moments of youth . . . never to return, and –

BEATRICE. – and remembering makes us gentler people?

ADAM. Perhaps. It's easier to forgive and hope to be forgiven.

They drink on in silence for a while.

That silence haunts these poems, and gives them a stark honesty which touches the reader. His poems to his first-born son, and later to his daughter, warning her about the snares of the world, are naked. They may not have the cadences of a practised poet; sometimes the demands of rhyming lead him astray; sometimes the diction is a little more Pre-Raphaelite than he would allow himself in a play. It hardly matters: they have their own music, they are their own evidence:

> We have our own mistakes to live with
> Learn from
> Who are we to offer help, alleviation
> When ourselves we scour the past
> Investigate each detail
> That we suffer
> Searching for that whisper in *our* ear
> Of hope, a little joy, some consolation?

There is anger in the long poem 'Abuse not words', warning demagogues of the Left (it could equally apply to the Right) that their macho, militant language disavows the very principles they stand for:

> Brothers. Momentary militants
> Perhaps, whose words can dip
> No deeper than their pocket's discontent.
> The cheap linguistic cuts you take
> Build no utopian avenues but soon unmake
> Where once stood
> Your lovely dreams of brotherhood.
>
> Abuse not words.

There is East End reminiscence, Petticoat Lane energy recalled, happiness sweet as bagels, but no more resistant to jackboot Time – 'And did the holy lamb of God / Turn happiness to fear?'

14

Above all, though, these are poems of quietness. If the texts of his plays require robust voices, these poems, especially the recent ones, harvested from three-score and ten years of innocence and experience, 'whisper in our ear'.

M.K., September 2007

PROLOGUE

This need to write poetry

This need to write poetry
A dangerous need
Like hankering for youth
Pining for Beatrice
Buoying muscles for
Perpetual momentum
An impossible need.

I know the traps
I list them
Pin them in my side
I bleed with cautions.
These:

Spirit,
At moments capable
Of poet-passion
Feels
Poetic
But
Poet-passion does not poet make.

What can we do
Poor those-of-us who feel
But O for whom
The world dissolves not
Into images of poetry?

We throb with melody
Yet no voice sings.
True poets pity us.

We could
(The demagogue is in us all)
We could
Evolve a theory for ourselves
Accommodating
The sad poverty of our muse,
Say:
'It is enough to scan
To rhyme
To fluently control the vowel
The pace
The length of line
Alliterate with modesty
Be clear be clear
Simplicity is all
Let's call the spade a spade
Communicate no ambiguity.'

We could.

We could
Announce sufficiency in that,
Create a school
Delineate a dogma
Dignify ineptitude
We could do that.
We do it with so much
Of our inadequate lives.

But poetry is not
The writing of words
With faint lilts
The tilting of prose
Discreetly into rhythm
No!

It is a falling of the world
Into its jealous shape
It is assembling vividly
The parts, the words
Which mercifully light up the dark
And shape with images
The meaning of the moment.

Images pierce hearts
Convey time's birth and death
And tell that
What lives beautifully
Speaks sadness
What is compared
Explains,
Not what described.

Poets are blessed.
The rest of us
Are animals of prose.

YOUTH AND AGE

I kissed a girl

I kissed a girl when I was a kid
And cuddled her curls as a man did
Said she was she and I was I
And learned what lessons she had to give.

I had a girl when I was young
Taught my lips and limbs to sing
Gave me her breasts to hide my head
And we went heel over heather dancing.

A nimble, wicked nurse came after
Nursed my numbness into laughter
We loved on music fed on air
And strode through nights without fear.

I loved a girl her limbs were long
We wrapped each other as the world sung
And spun and spun
Dizzy and fierce and young.

I have a waitress O so warm
Her lips are moist and honey juiced
I kiss her ephemeral love in the alley
From first star till dawn.

And I know when she will fade there are more
To mate and betray at the marriage door
I'll be strong and I will dare
Silly, eager and unsure.

But one day will emerge another
When fear is fled and all's in place
And she I'll love till my world dies
Though I cling for ever and ever.

Old men fear slipping

Old men fear slipping on stones
The treachery of friends
Losing focus
Sad memories
Sticks and broken bones.

Long-legged youth striding
Stir their regret for time wasted
Lovely things that were
As well as what was missed and meant.

Catch children leaping
And their heart leaps
Old men fear pain there
Unannounced embarrassment.

Old men fear slips of mind
The terrible trips of regret
Sleeping past their station
Loss and all they would forget
But cannot for the vivid pain
Of remembering again and again.

Old men fear ridicule
Sadness in their children's eyes
The counting of days
Tastes gone
The inability to run and run
The pity of their wives.

Old men fear never waking again.

You love me now

You love me now but wait until
Upon my lips you heed no more
And in my arms you lie and scatter
Lovely dreams you struggled for

And in my eyes no longer see
The child that you were before.
Upon my heart you'll lay your head
And know of things that matter more.

Then shall the arm's length of your kiss
Turn in me all that was to stone
And from a carelessness of touch
Will I know love has gone.

Ah, hard is love and soft its ties
And soft the contours of our lives
Not all your woman's winter tears
Shall take you back among sweet sighs.

You love me now but wait until
You've loved my thighs a thousand times.

Old men forget

Old men forget and fail, poor things.
They stumble over steps
Where confidence once strode
And fumble where
Resolve rode with the best of them.
They have no need
To make decisions now
No power to do and lead.

Old men miscalculate endurance
And their age,
Chase youth with legs no longer brisk
Tempt heart to love beyond itself
Imagine time has stopped
Around the forty mark.
Old men forget the gap between
Ambition and lapsed energy.

Old men have heads that can't quite
Understand inexorable time,
There is a discrepancy they fail
To pull together, comprehend.

Their eagerness has bled,
They've seen it once they've seen it twice
The going's gone.

Old men regret the marks
They've failed to leave behind,
Mistakes so stupid that their wrinkles
Blush with memory,
And hope has fled.

Come love me, I

Come love me, I
Will bear your ways
And in your eyes become
The longed-for dream
Of balmy days
Where paradise and paradox
Sit easily as one.

Love, come and I
With all you cannot guess in me
Will shape in you and you in me
As wind to wave and wave to rock
Let love lock fast the paradox
Of paradise and tyranny.

Come, love, to me
And flesh my side
Where men have slashed
And shamed pride
That I with stubbornness too long denied.
Together we will teach and learn
What each desires
Before love's seeds
In paradise are sown
To harvest needs,
And the heart expires.

Come, love, say why
You're filled with fear,
Your heart has gazed into my eyes
And deep-sea dived
My mysteries
Drawn tears enough.

I tire of goodbyes.
Your fears are rough
They frighten me.

It is not wise always to be wise
Or to resist love's tyranny.

Old men fart

Old men fart, forget names, snore
And aren't for loving any more.
What must be done?
Discard them when they bore?
Where? There are no rubbish dumps
For OAP used bones
Unless you're contemplating old-age homes
Where sitting bums get sore
And memory doesn't serve them any more.

Old men repeat themselves
Forget their yesterdays
But not the past.
What scant memory lasts
Is filled with days
Of youth and wicked ways.
But what was said and done
An hour ago like mist becomes.
They mourn they mourn
The passing of their moons and suns.

Old men pee pants
Flirt beyond their means, falter.
Once they made the day happen
Now they alter
Nothing.
Nor do they care
As cared they did about
The daft old world
Once.
Now, daft old men
They look askance
And place a blustering blame
Where they can or dare
Regardless of the relevance.

It was a time of feasts and weddings

It was a time of feasts and weddings.
Everyone we knew was pairing.
Partners sprang to life at parties
And chance meetings.
No suspicions, no withheld smiles
Egos at their lowest
Trust and expectations – buoyant.
We believèd what was uttered.
Dress expressed a love of cut and cloth
The crotch was hinted at
Not brazenly defined.
Even spring came earlier
And O that balmy summer.

Passion was around all right
But pressed where it belonged.
We were tender with one another
Forgave each other mistakes.
The winds blew in autumn
We wept for dead parents
Yet there was no bleak distress.
A sadness for all things which pass,
Of course
But winter held no terrors.
When spring came again
We would all still be young.

Old men cry out

Weep for them the old men weep
For them and theirs
The pain of all their passing years.

Old men cry out in sleep
Dream vivid dreams of youth.
They cannot keep down
The pain of passing years,
Sleeping or awake catch up.
The young man has raced on.
They cannot stem the dream's tears.

Weep for them the old men weep
For them and theirs
The pain of all their passing years.

Old men sit wondering at themselves
Caught by the cunning silence
Of the spider,
Misled, their heads confused, spinning.
Clogged by time's web they feel betrayed,
No one had told them time moves
No one had warned.
Who knows such things
When youth is not a dream
And the girls sing and the blood sings?

Weep for them the old men weep
For them and theirs
The pain, the pain of all their passing years.

The first child

For Lindsay Joe

He will give me kisses and the cream off the milk
And pull down clouds to warm my ears,
He will touch my lips with a tongue of silk
And sing away my tears.

Do not make me weep with that look in your eyes
I will give you honey, little boy, and a bear,
You can pester me with your 'whys'.
There will be sunlight all year.

He will give me cuddles and sleepless nights
And moan with his long growing pains.
What will he dream these first nights?
He will call me his own name.

I will give you kisses and the cream of my time
And a penny to buy black sweets.
Your wide laugh will last longer than mine
As you grow in the streets.

He will give me kisses and the cream off the milk
And reasons why he was born,
And I will feel the touch of his tongue of silk
Long after his youth is gone.

For Dusty

The pain of flesh this night touched
Intensifies my love but must
Defuse my joy
That flesh shall dust become.

Unbearable to hold you knowing
What I clasp succumbs
Will heap and blow away
Held back by nothing in my power.

Upon your love depend I and
Within your shape I flower
And soundly sleep.
But one day

Where I link and lock
Will crumble. How impossible
It seems. Absurd that this
I hold will curve with time away.

The stumbling age

We've reached the age of stumbling
And sad uncertain thoughts,
Hold on to banisters and worn beliefs
Trip over dark suspicions
Lurking through the years
Creeping free now because
There's no time left for lies
Denial or pretence.

Our step is wobbly
Socks and courage threadbare.
We've lost the skip, the dream
The dare, the leap two at a time.

We've reached the age of stumble when
Because the hours left are few
We doubt what we have done
Feel guilt for what was badly done
Mourn all that remains undone.

I marvel at these things

I marvel at these things:
Who conceived the wheel?
Where is he remembered?
Who first gazed and gazed at the seed
Upon whom dawned in that dawn
Here all begins?
Who shepherded
Then twisted his intelligence
Round the sheep's back
To spin warmth against chaotic storms?
I marvel at the unravelling of chaos
I marvel at these things.

I marvel at these things:
Who dared pluck the first fruit
Risked the unknown tastes of life
Took courage and fire in his hands
Regarded rocks with fantasies
He could not know he possessed
But guessed gold was there
Smote steel, struck coal
And greedily perceived the gem?
Which is the man,
Is he named
Who combed seas
Understood there was a task to be done
And he could of all strange creatures
He could?
I marvel at these things.

All my years before me

For Della and Ralph

I want to be singing again
Round fires with friends
Loud, full of harmony
Breath in my lungs
And all my years before me

I want again those I knew
And talked with all night through
Discovering the world
Argument on my lips
And all my years before me

I want not to have read
Dead Souls, Bovary
Hardy, Lawrence, *Orlando*
Fathers and Sons
John Donne
Penguins stacked ready
And all my years before me

Give me my first love
Dreams and courage again
Expectation in my parents' eyes
Hopes, promise, lost youth
And all my years before me

I ache for the dead
Long for my mother's laugh
My father's songs
My sister's wedding feast

War letters from abroad her husband wrote
Telling me I was talented
Intelligent, my voice had broken.
I want each family event again
With all my years before me.

Old boats

My chest creeks like an old boat
Left behind, long forgotten.
The rotten hulk
Of past glories and adventure
Courage, fears
Heave on tired tides.
The wind sighs
The timber soaks up tears.

We'll sail no more to Byzantium
Nor challenge storms
Round rough capes
Nor ride high the stern salt waves
Whom nothing halts.

And yet within this bony barrel
Beats youth's dream.
The young man cannot comprehend
Erosion, rust
The superseding thrusts of power
The blunting of lust
The loss of steam.

The sails are down
And threadbare,
Gulls croak
Glide here and there.
Wings sing.
The old frown
Oh, there is little left
To catch the wind of things.

I was maidenhead hunted

I was maidenhead hunted
From twelve years on
But twelve years on found no man
For this hotheaded maiden to sit upon.

The evening sky has a pink hue
As the shy sun lowers its gaze
My breasts sigh as I wonder why
I never understood men's ways.

My maidenhead has long since gone
Squandered with indifference, waste
Responding to plaintive pleas
And glibly offered with wanton haste.

The days are short the maiden old
Melancholy regrets fall upon stone
Who will look after the cooled hothead
Now that the hotheaded maiden lives alone?

This poem is called

I was young
not long ago

THREE POEMS FOR
MY DAUGHTER
TANYA JO

on her twenty-first birthday

from her father on his fiftieth

One

Take pause, love
Take in deep breaths of everything
That heart, love
Has many parts to sing
But tuned and toned for you
Not cleft and sharp for you
Too loving thing.

Take time, love
To find the words will lock your thoughts
Name feelings their right name.
Claim grace, love
Stand back.
Each view is different
From a different place.
Take pause
Sweet, gentle love.

Remember, love
Two bloods run tense in you.
Your stock is mixed
And so of course
You will be vilified
In your long life,
Thrown down
Again, again.
Let them mock
Let them, love.

Gently, careful, easy, love
Breathe deep,
Delight in friends, music
Youth's magic dance
But do not bare
Your breast to all
Nor turn from the heart's silence.

Be sometimes still, sometimes alert
Your heart must burn
But oh, your heart must not be hurt.
Go gently, sweetly, love.

Two

I would take upon me all for you
Pain me your pain
Your sadness bear
Your tears weep
Mistakes make mine
And shames keep
Deep in my old soul.
Oh that I could for you.

But I cannot
There it is that life
In which one day
You will be no one's daughter.

Prepare, daughter
For what I cannot
Do and die for you
Though I would for you
Forever for you
But there it is
I cannot for you.

I wish that only had been passed
The finest of my genes to you
Irresolute ones lost
The foolish spent
Bewildered ones destroyed
Those of weakness,
Cowardice, fear,
Foolhardiness, despair,
Dispersed.
But there it is
They were not
You have all.

Everything and all
That in you rages,
Hurts, intoxicates –
Concoct with what spice and pain
And spare imagination
I have endowed you,
The best around you,
I cannot for you
Though I would all all for you.

Three

You will walk streets empty
As a broken heart
Part with friends become frost
Who once spoke honeydew, sparkled.
Freeze the cost
Go on.
Mourn friends lost
But go on! Graft sad memories
Upon fresh starts
But go on!

You will love love's leaps
Lithe as young athletes,
Fail like the runner by mere seconds
Train for what cannot be
Break your fond limbs
Upon passionate false hearts.
Go on! Breathe deep into your lungs
Hope's bizarre alchemy.

You will hear shrieks
Of righteous furies
Exhortations, claims of priests
Emotional, religious bullies
Who possess *the* truth
And have no appetite for
Awkward queries.
Go on. Walk past.
Ignore weak minds
Declaiming urgent words.
Nonsense seduces. Beware the signs.

You will savour lives
Like cheese on a good grocer's board
Mellow, sharp, spiced, sometimes high.
You will dine with gods
Golden and dark
Drink sweet melancholy

Eat humble pie.
Feast on! Scorn the dull.
Plunge teeth into the best
Spit out the bland.
Tastes may betray
But feast on!
I meant you born for a wonderland.

FIVE POEMS FOR
HAROLD PINTER

I favoured her

I favoured her, she him
And him to whom her love fell
Fell elsewhere, what

She said, is love
If love like this strays
Here and there, what

She said, must the heart
Hold, discard, if ways
And means mean little, what

She said, signing
The warrant for love's death,
Was the alternative, what?

The actor dies

So, old time was torn away from him.
We sat. Slurped coffee. Wondered
Should we carry on? To rehearse what?
Without him? Unthinkable.
He filled space for us all.
A hammy fart but full of fine
Concern ham actors have off-stage.

I learned from him good things and bad.
To hide my vanity, convey meaning
Laugh at myself, upstage the dire.
I caught his sonorous tones like flu.
He was Irish. Made audiences weep.
Which made him smile. 'Manipulate them, boy
Is all I do,' he said.

He feared derision. Loved to be loved.
Never played with fire. Took risks
With emotions only behind make-up.

I think he knew he would die soon.

Count ten

Count ten. Then
Count ten again.
That way is time measured
Death denied.
Each measures time
His own way – coffee breaks
Rejections, instalments
On the car.

Count blessings. Then
Count them again.
That way is heart fooled
Honed, toned down.
Each fools his shadow
Shadows his dreams
Stalking himself
In circles
In circles move shadows.

Count circles. Then
Count them again.
That way are trees, time
Honed expectations
Measured, laid out.

She waits, he hesitates

She waits, he hesitates
He has the fear of male
She the female's certitude.

Where he comes from she went.
What he abandoned she adored.

Adoring, he hesitates
Why she waits he cannot fathom.
She is familiar with such men.
Familiar, she waits.

In between the waiting hesitating play
Is silence. His uncertainty
Her contempt, spread like calm
Before the storm.

'Form is all.' Finally she broke
The Carthusian pact.
'All is known
Predictable, banal.'

'If all is form, what,' he asked,
'Is there in you for me to hold?'
He waits. She hesitates.

Between the waiting hesitating play
Sides change. The certitude
Is his. The fear hers.

Links

Hand me up my heart
Is up and down we go
Sweet love of mine
Is all you need not
Question any more
Or less is more
We want the less we need
Is mother to intent
To make it permanent
Manent . . . manent . . . manent . . .

'STORMS' AND OTHER POEMS

Storms

For Lisa Appignanesi

The days of leaping from bed
To witness fierce storms rage
Are done.

Electric battles wake the night
Dreams are disturbed
Sleep broken.

Once it was fun. I'd stand
Against my mother's warnings
By the fragile glass
Waiting for the dark
To be illuminated
The flashing traced in strange shapes
Always pleasing, always a surprise.

I was unafraid
Nothing could strike me
I could face anything
The world might threaten with.

There I stood confronting rage and angry power
Such arbitrary splendid rage and power
Un-intimidated, feeling blessed
Immune, immortal
I could catch the storm's fury in my hands
Turn it back, make evil burn.
That's how it was.

Now – who dared guess at such change –
Now I lie anxious with eyes closed
The flash filtering through tight lids
Counting the seconds between lightning
And the crack of thunder
Following for sure.

That's how it is.
Who dared guess!

The well has lost its winder

For Tarn

The well has lost its winder
Before the sowing is done;
We shall not see the trees leave
Nor the spring come.

Nor any first sigh of the seasons
Shall run through our hair.
The meadow has lost its children
And the house is bare.

Can you see we built an island
Among the fields of corn
Window and brickwork
Patched the house before it was born?

We tended with loving and hammers
Responded to every call.
Now we must move away again
And the house lose its lord.

The wind will taste of the winter
And the waters of rain run soft
But we will lament that the tilly lamp
No longer burns for us.

There was a time my bones knew

There was a time my bones knew how to sleep
My head lay soft not smug but quite content
With the day, unafraid tomorrow
Might hold disappointment.

There was a time my body eased in shapes
Of peace and folds of wonderment
All curled and cuddled trustingly
Not nervous, drained or tense but nicely spent.

There was a time of love and sleep
Safe and secure that the long days meant
For me and me alone would never end.
And in the morning ah! the world would be there for my
    enjoyment.

Dormant dreads rise to their own
Driving the last of my sap into bewilderment.
Now I fear gnarled blossom filling me
With smells of autumn and disenchantment.

Of photographs and albums

For Roger Frith, poet

How old we grow and sparse.
Invent the mirror to remind,
The camera to record
The grin, rich laughter for
That skin of celluloid.
We hope to laugh again
At patient scrapbooks
Waiting for decades to pass.

What scrutiny we give to images long done with,
What manic measuring
Of wrinkled glance
Collapsed breast and hooded eye,
The young shoots at our side
Who'll grow to be there when we've gone.

Carefully we pin on walls
The glossy charts and graphs
That measure failure
Stolen happiness, decline,
Sometimes success,
And pine and pine
To see how years
And relatives have fled
And what we have become –
Sad faces bleached
Of loveliness and loss.

Who could guess
After so much was done
And undone.
So many dead.

The confidence of boughs

Some
Terrified caught sinning with false feeling
Expose none
Risk no emotion
Chance no love
Drain their generosity.
Contempt withers them.

Why
We wonder
Watching them curl their lips
Like stricken leaves
Brown with distaste for the earth's nourishment.
The soil too rich perhaps
Their veins too thin?

Others feel all
Soak up everything
Weather winters
Survive frostbite
Dare blossom each time they must.

But some
Terrified caught sinning with false feeling
Resist their natural cycles
Disdain like a disease spreads,
The confidence of boughs to grow
Is stunted
The bark cracked
The dew soured
The sap stemmed.

If we parted

If we parted
Would we soon become strangers
Shy, withdrawn
Passion paled, spirit lean
Though we had fattened upon intimacies
Through five and twenty years or more
What would such parting mean?

If we parted
Would there be malevolence
Acrimony, angers
Divisions of children and the marriage spoils
Would friendship not linger
Long enough to forgive and remember
Our ecstasies, our joys?

I betray she betrays they betray
You disappoint
We disappoint
All disappoint
Thus the grammar of love
Friends fail friends.
Fathers forsake sons
Daughters drift
Mothers die lonely and bitter bitter bitter

If we parted
Would no cloud part for us
Permitting one pure ray
To lighten the failed landscape of our love
Which though neglected now and sad
We once had feasted sweetly from
Nourished greedily at times
Laughed and built our hopes upon
Drank deeply its dark wines?
Not one not *one* warm ray?

If we parted
Would it take so little to become strangers
Nothing remain
No besotted passion left
Nothing nothing nothing but pain?

The clouds are low

For Maggie Drabble on her birthday

The clouds are low the clouds are low
They press.

My mother was the same
'The clouds are low,' she'd fret
'They press I feel oppressed.'

When the clouds were low and grey
Anxiously I'd ring her twice
'Alright, Mum?'
'Alright. Why?'
'The clouds are low the clouds are low.'
'If you're worried, come!'

So I'd go
We'd sit in misery, and grin
To be such helpless victims
Of the passing clouds
Which hover grey
And flatten thought
Bleach colour from the day
Bleed sunless the heart,
Cautious times of patient pain
When appetites are listless
Longing seems uncouth
Mistakes forever
Each blemish a mark of Cain
And oh those doubts of self
Such unarguable truth.

I need champions

I need champions to gather
Like flies round my sweat
Smelling of apples and cider
Buzzing me on
Drowning doubts,
I'll dig endlessly then
Prepare earth to receive seeds
Remove boulders
Grow all manner of strange tall trees
Coloured shrubs,
And with fragmented stones
Build walls.

But to sweat in chill winds
Brings fever and ache
Drained bones can lift nothing
The greedy couch grass creeps
Triumphant through my fragile roots
Smug weeds flourish
Nothing grows to be gathered, bunched
Offered to the table,
The vase is empty
No fragrance floats in
The gardener is frozen out
Encased in cold loathing.
Only young suns can burn him free
Bring on the sweet sweat that once
Smelt of apples, and made flies
Dance drunk on his cider skin.

Insomnia

For Pamela Howard

Tell me, reassure me.
Would I drift easy into sleep
Were passion spent?
Soft-toe myself to dream
Were nothing to disturb me
Stir me, thrill, absorb me?

Tell me. Reassure me.
If the heart, the flesh, the mind
Ceased bubbling
Would slumber sweetly come instead
And would I find my troubling calmed?
Reassure me – if the plunder came
Of all that made me
Makes and breaks me
Guides my hand, and dazzles
What imagination I was born with
Would insomnia like mist arise
And nights not sleepless be the same?

Tell me. Reassure me.
Were I to render void my being
Strip my life of what surprises and disturbs it
Could I soundly sleep again?
Drift easy into sleep again?

Lines for a soldier

I am born
I am taught
I grow things, I build things
I marry
Have children
Teach them kindness
I am attacked
I defend
I am murdered
Burried
Mourned.

I look in the mirror

I look in the mirror
I am my mother
I look at my eyes
I see her sadness
I smile
She smiles
I laugh at myself
My foolishness
She mocks my posing and pretension
Laughs with me
At herself.

I look in the mirror
I am my mother
I see her love
I see her rage
I look in the mirror
Hear her brothers' tones
Their children's laughter
Struggles that go back
Beyond certificates
Of births and deaths and lineage.

Inebriated men and true

To all my children

You must not proffer honesty
Impossible!
You'll be misunderstood
Abused
By those who chained Prometheus.

You must not trust your heart around
Embarrassing!
Who was the friend
Misled
Said dare expose your vulnerability?

You must not down your cards
Unhug them from your chest
Beware!
To call a spade a spade
Becomes
The murderous tool they hack you with.

No one will thank you for a truth
That's merely yours,
Who do you think you are
Daring
To bring fire hot upon their heads?

Fierce, self-righteous foes await you
Judges lurk like pubs on every corner
Drunk with narrow certitudes
A pint of answers in their hands
Intoxicated eyes ablaze with self-contempt
And fear of your sobriety.

Who do you think you are
Trying to be honest
Confidently laying down your cards
A poker hand of spades
Your heart too good to be believed
When they and they alone
Are Jesus Christ's inebriated men and true?

LONGER POEMS

All things tire of themselves

On the occasion of my fiftieth birthday, 24 May 1982

All things tire of themselves
Be comforted be glad
Not only the singer's joy
But the demagogue's tongue
The revolutionary's fervour
All that makes love sad
And passion
Be comforted be glad.

Be comforted
That all things tire of themselves
For with recrimination, rancour,
Ease fierce longings for revenge
Small satisfactions of spite
Not only hope, despair also
And the night.
All tire tire of themselves
Be glad be comforted.

Be comforted.
Though confidence falters
Holy grails fade
And sin.
Contempt withers
The sneer dissolves
Bored cynics expire.
Unhappiness wearies also
And ranters wear their shrillness thin
All things all things tire of themselves
And passion.
Be comforted and glad.

Be comforted.
Though smiles fade
Aches weary
Weeping weeps itself to sleep.
Beloved melodies incessantly replayed
Collapse
Melt out of meaning
New words too loud and overused
Cease making sense
But silence, too
That tires of itself
The writing on the wall must speak.
Be comforted
All things all things
And passion.

Ah! How can that be we wonder?
How can such energy and joy
Come to an end? It does
And love
It does
And sweet faith chaos can be ordered
People reasoned
It does it does.
Childhood of childishness
Youth of certitude
Manhood of bravery
All things tire of themselves
Be comforted be glad.

Be comforted
Though sanity sweet sanity turns mad
Fury, too, must end
Mockery turn bleak
Be comforted be glad.
Who win tire of their winning streak
The heart must mend.

The city tires of its dreams
Evil of its tyranny
The long storm of its turbulence
All tires of itself
And passion.

Ah! can passion tire of itself?
Can that ever be, we wonder,
Happy with the heights
All images sharp and glowing
Language on edge
Our usage precise
Inventive, humour-bright
And all nerves ringing ringing?
Can it be
Such passion tires of itself?
It does it does
As all things do
Be glad be comforted.
And if madness follows
Will that, too, tire of itself?
Will all life rot
And metamorph itself
As all things do?
It will, it will
Be glad
Though no joy lasts
Pain lingers not.

Only this knowledge remains:
That all tires of itself
All recreates
Nothing sustains
But knowing this is so.

Now go. Life waits.
Be glad be comforted.

Vain image

A blackbird
Intermittently throughout the day
Throws himself against the window of my house.

What he sees he cannot reach
What bars his way he cannot see.

The tiny brain learns nothing
From the pain, the jar, the shock
His minute frame receives
With each huge futile hurl.

He fails to comprehend transparent walls.

Conflicting fact is
To his slight sense
Unknown
Surely what is seen can be touched?
Through glass is food to eat
Dry rest from rain
Comfort different
From the frozen bark
The wormless earth
Unpredictable winds
And the mad sly days
Of wet winter skies?

Or is he vain
A narcissistic flutterer
Aching to clasp
That other breast beating to know him
An amazing mirrored image
Loving itself
Pointlessly flapping wings at nothing
Bar this cruel crystal cage?

Day after day they fly at one another
Lovers never to be
Not even friends,
Doomed to gaze
At what each sees each sees
Is there,
Two selves
Two daft deceived demented things
Never to scythe the air as one
Never to know
To comfort
Not even meet.

When I return

When I return
Calculate my welcome
Be deliberate with surprise
Show you have observed
Each step I took towards your arms
Confidently care for me
Above all else – love.

Do these things
Do them
And I will rekindle
Old dreams for you.

Track my way with arrows on the street
Loving slogans on the walls
Flowers at the porch.
Light candles for the dark.
Weigh, sift, and simmer food
Reteach my tongue its tastes
Let music seep through half-closed doors
Arrange what I have cherished
To remind me how
I cherished without doubts – once
Thinking it was good
The beauty men made.

Do these things
Do them
That I, too, may have the strength
To calculate surprise for you.

Remember my hungers
Quench my thirsts in these dry times
Line my blood and kin to kiss my lips.

I'm swollen with fears
Terror has stolen courage
Freshen me then
Reassure me then
Bleed my fears
My eyes will be clouded
My pores clogged with disgust
My skin dried with disappointment
My hair grey with anger.
Prepare scented waters and white sheets
Stiff with your habits of attention.
Attend to me
The years have been cruel
To my cruelty
Patient with my thin ability
To learn the lessons they were meant to learn.
Don't cry for what has gone
Instead greet, love, forgive
Tell me how I am welcomed back
That time is left to do much
Before the mortal doors close
Stern, inevitably.

Do these things
Then listen to the laughter
The singing
See the pledges in my eyes.

Do these things
Do them
I will learn new arts
You will forget pain.

It does not come easy

It does not come easy knowing
What must be done for happiness,
Like shifting and re-shifting in bed
Through restless nights
When wide-awake memories
Doubts and shameful enmities
Reverse the time of day.
Sleep eludes
Confusion upon discomfort
Disorder like a teenage space.

There is no certain, single wriggle
Into the right position
For peace of mind.

Change your partner, unpick
Your marriage, friendships
Tested reasonable convictions,
All those details of a life
Which made you.

Unmake them if you can
Unknit the cosy patterns
If you dare!

You sit up in bed
Punch a pillow or two
Slough off a woollen blanket
Shed pyjamas hoping for cool thoughts
Imagine you thirst for water
Reach for the glass – empty!
You have already drunk from it.

On your back, your stomach, foetal,
Nothing helps
You do not know how to stretch or curl.

Restless you retrace the careful years.
Skein after skein had been wound in readiness
For a rich life,
A modest though not dull pattern chosen
You knew the stitches –
Purl, plain, cable, moss.
So – what went wrong?
You check.
Instructions had been sensibly observed,
Along the way stitches were dropped
You do not remember where or how.
Stitches will always drop.
Too late to return
Such holes cannot be hidden
Fixed forever now.
Something will always be missing.

Helplessly you lie
Propped against pillows
Your knitter's hands surrendered
To your Buddha stomach
Concentrating on the spaces in your life
Waiting to be struck by insights
Or oblivion.

What on earth can you do with this heap?
Sleep, hum, count yourself out, reknit?

Reknit!
What is the point?
Your head may be alert
Your needle fingers nimble
But your eyes are out of focus
To distinguish plain from purl.
The heap will be the same
Merely unstrung from its normal shape.
You have forgotten how to cast on, besides.
Nor did you ever like the colour of the wool.

Somehow sleep comes
Impossible to recall when
Somehow the fevered mind, exhausted,
Clutched that thought which struck you out, cold
Unexpectedly.
Somehow your flesh had strewn itself
Across sheets
Found rest.
Somehow.

And dreams come.

Dreams come
Bringing with them
From where and God knows why
The loved faces
Of disappointed parents
Tender, aching, gone forever.
Streets in which upon-a-long-ago
You once were happy.
Maybe.

At which you weep and wake with tears.

Or you have dreamt an awful deed
Dealt in drugs
Inexplicably committed murder.
You worry for the children
Who will suffer shame.
It is a dream of angst and tawdry crimes
Deluged with guilt, remorse
Suppressed and so distressing
You resist it
Swim and thrash away from it
Returning to the land of living
Saturated with relief and sweat.
The dream, unbearably, is clear:
You failed them.

Sleeping or awake – no difference.
Neither tells you what to do for happiness.
Like chess the permutations
For wrong moves are endless.
With each loss the spaces grow
The bleakness multiplies.
Decline is geometric.

It is even hard to know what brief
You should present yourself
To live this best of all possible lives
This holy, hapless quest.

So many have strange strategies.
Not you.
Amazed, you watch them gallop
Through campaigns
Competing to beat this and that
Flailing opinions here and there
Striking left and right to carve a space
For their voracious appetites, ambitions
Righteous expectations.
Not you.
What went wrong?
You moved about the world
Made yourself a little interesting
Been distracted and impressed
By remarkable women
Seen history in galleries and ruins
Marvelled at the industry of thousands
Incredibly revealed in jewellery and lace
Porcelain and sword
Carvings, tapestries
The woven clothes of Emperors and Queens.

The gifted tempered who you are
You paid them homage
Eagerly expressed your gratitude
For their light in dark times.

So, what, what went wrong?

Your problem was
You could not find a blueprint for that patchwork quilt,
The one that safely might despatch you off to sleep.
You try again
You slip from slippers into bed
And pull the old day
Over wide-awake and restless eyes.
Nothing from the past assembles.

Happiness is a craft, perhaps.
It must be learnt, perhaps.
You have not finished
The long apprenticeship, perhaps.

You lie in bed where discontent
Amazed and sultry
Crouched in wait to ambush you
Into the parched and melancholy night
Asking yourself
But what is left to learn?
Which move?
What tactic now?

'Death alone solves all,' you mumble
Hoping to dream stranger stratagems than other men,
To pacify the pain
Drift out of this day's tribulations
Hoping, hoping to by-pass
The prodding heart of things.
'Death alone solves all.'

The banal thought
Like the cheap song
Settles you.

All will be revealed
In that last damp clay-cold bed
Where the sad somnambulist
Is lowered to his lonely sleep
And where alongside his forlorn
Forgotten corpse they mix
The great, the happy
Every dull, bled dilettante
And innocent,
The heroes, martyrs, craftsmen
All mixed
With the sublime,
The endless knitters
Players of chess
The unfulfilled dead.

Mistakes writ large

The streets are filled with people
Who have made mistakes
Writ large upon their face.

Some push prams
Some sport stubble on their chin
Some look as though their lives
Are daily wakes.

They deadly gaze
With resignation in their eyes
Having lost last chances
They were never born to win
Knowing that they can't amaze
Affect, control,
Fearful of their neighbours' glances
Wishing it was end of days.

How can they be helped?
What whisper in their ear
Would waken them
Give hope
Eradicate the daily fear
They daily creep from sleep to meet
And fail to overcome?

Can they be told persuasively
A better life exists to greet them
If they persevere, persist?
They overwhelm us with their misery
Despair
As we walk past
Utterly aware
That what we whisper cannot last
Unless we take them home as family.

But family they're not.
Worse – they might despise
Our rhythms
What we stand for
Even that we care,
Confused by our concern
Suspicious of our interest
Too numbed by their despair.

We have our own mistakes to live with
Learn from.
Who are we to offer help, alleviation
When ourselves we scour the past
Investigate each detail
That we suffer
Searching for that whisper in *our* ear
Of hope, a little joy, some consolation?

Flight AF 4590
(Concorde crashed 25 July 2000)

For my youngest son, Dan

Built on safety speed and style
They said.

The dead were Germans
Tourists who had planned
A lifetime's dream
Concorde Paris to New York
MS Deutchland from
New York to Sydney
Through the Panama Canal
Via Ecuador full steam ahead
To the Olympic games.

One hundred died
Nine crew
Five on the ground
We do not know their names.

We only know they said goodbye
To children parents friends
Who wished them happy holiday
Safe flight take care and see you soon.

They were not given time
To enjoy the legendary speed
No barrier of sound was broken
Just their terrified tense backs
No time for cries or token prayers
Only the fulfilment of unspoken fears.

Now I need God's lies
The believer's shameless consolation
Of God's strange, mysterious ways.

Any lie will serve
About creation's mystery
Dying and hereafter
I will take it all unquestioningly
There is no strength in me
To reason
Sift meaning from mad chance
Make sense where
Emptiness exists.

The day following
My son, Dan, flew with Phoebe
Three years old, his daughter.
Each perished passenger
Was them.
I kissed my dears safe flight
Take care and see you soon.

What lie would help accept?
What consolation could console?
How cruel of God
His will to do.
What glory
Oh, what power and cruelty
To arbitrarily
Give birth and take.

I need but do not understand
His lies and wherefores.
No! Oh, no!
Them gone
This everything I am would break.

There goes the year

There goes the year
Wrapped in dead leaves
Warped and burned copper
From hanging on against winds
That would insist time is come
Go, go! Leave hold! Be done
And satisfied.

Satisfied?
I look back at what budded
In those crisp seductive weeks
Of watery sun and tentative green.
Does it seem the garden blossomed?
Trees fulfilled their pledge?
The hedge its promise?
The shrub its lambent glean?

Well, the old cycle turned
Dutifully producing what it must,
When winter moved beyond
Its cold quota of dismal days
It was accommodated – as pain.

And, when spring smiled her turn on stage
Dropping her curtain before we applauded
All we felt and longed for,
She blushed.
And the cycle shrugged, resigned.
It happens that way.

But not content
The winter brazenly returned before its time
Under the sun's nose
Bewildering us with chills that came
From where, unjustly where, and why?

The cycle shrugged again
Again accommodating shabby misery.

Be satisfied with what, then?
There goes another year
Tossed carelessly by winds blown not by me
Or mine or those concerned.
There swiftly goes another enigmatic year
I hardly came to know.
Wait! Wait for me!
Let me catch up, collect, attach
These changes to myself
Let me absorb the seasons' shocks
Of unpredictability.

But no! Go, go the years
Leaf after leaf
Blind wanton wind upon blind
Whether there be gales, sunlight
No winds at all
And oh I cannot shrug
Accommodate or be resigned.

Time parts memory

Time parts memory. The mind opens
Old alleys in new lights. I beckon
The green boy back with his laughter,
Laugh with him at his beloved days
When wars went past his careless sense
And meant nothing more than searchlights
Shelter smells and fire-blitzed skies.

They were days to dream about
When bombs and dying fell to others,
The world was wrong, he was right
And a liberal mother slapped no laws upon him.
The slum held him, lapped like a loving dog
His tin-can-copper days in harmless streets
And playground-boys of bad ways and truant times.

Where are those lovely boys? Age lost them down
The Lane of stalls, melted them from sight or
Blighted them; faces pale now, smiles gone now
Died with vows beneath the marriage canopy.
Sweet are rituals synagogue can sing.

Where are those lovely boys? Gone from their mothers,
Gone from toiling Talmud Torahs.
Mourned by masters endlessly teaching,
They burn at the stake of their sad ambitions
Having traded brave youth for 'better times',
Prepared to barter back again those 'better times'
For games and bravery and alleys of deceit.

They say only the aged die of nostalgia, yet
Still young, I lift ten years to resurrect The Lane,
Gas-lamps, fog and chestnuts roasted
On a shovel gingerly held above hot coals.
The Lane of their hearts scream with loss
In the dim-lit streets where lovely boys
Once bounced over toys and ruins
Left by wars of storming fathers.

Regard the names on walls:
Wentworth Street, Fashion Street
Flower-and-Dean Street where
Bed-ridden with arthritis lies the *bobba-mine*
Who always found a farthing in her purse
From paradise beneath her pillow.

Regard the little bastard everybody thought I was
Playing marbles in his aunties' playground-like-a-prison
Full of parents watching sons and daughters
Safely passing days where neither cars nor crooks
Threatened hop-scotch, skipping, cricket
And the furtive corner kiss.

The Lane was coloured fruit and shmutter stalls in gutters
Manned by bearded fathers of forgotten times;
The skull cap covered their respect to God.
Few of them sold their soul; their hymns
Were banked between the Bible's pages,
Prayers now taken up by sons as old as they.

But that was then when Sabbath-joy by-passed
Pale heretics abandoning pale roots,
Cramped thoughts and suffocating skies
Where God was challenged and idealists sang
Socialism on the boxes of their dreams.
How May Day swam with banners bright
A memorable event for kids
Amid floods of argument.

When will he hear again such passionate protests
Borne shoulder-high through
Poverty and pride?
These were comrades brave and true
Taking the boy to certainty with song, strikes,
Stern orders for unity
And undying love in the pockets of their humanity.

Where will he find again the ardour
Age wrenched from playmates in his school?
Was it frightened wives who lead them back to safety?
Was it banks stagnated hope?
And did imagination freeze in ways
Undreamt of, never stored against
A dull happiness not bargained for
Way back in balmy days of daring and bravado?
And did the holy lamb of God
Turn happiness to fear?

Regard how one boy burned too bright for wives
And sailed to foreign lands
Where laughter was not scorned.
One happy boy did burn
Abandoning a life lived many times
Before his birth bounced in a cot
And caged his curls and mother's eyes.

He bears the spirit, Jew that he is, of dreams
And dares to be the equal
Of his gentile neighbour
Troubled though that neighbour be
Who hounds his trust.
He bears the stigma of a history
That Christ forgives and Christians
Can't forget, and laughs and loves
And cries alone among pale stones of sighs.

Time parts memory. New paths are lain.
New years leap up that cannot be lived down.
Hope is naïve yet cannot be denied
And spring, thank God, turns age to innocence again.

'tin-can-copper' was a children's street game.
'The Lane' is Petticoat Lane.
'Talmud Torahs' literally means 'Bible Schools'.
'Flower-and-Dean Street' no longer exists.
'bobba-mine' means 'my grandmother'.
'shmutter' means 'third-rate garments'.

Abuse not words

For the Left

Abuse not words they will betray.

Treacherous are they
Who hurl their tired jargon into winds
For winning praise and following.

Abuse not words to catch with vulgar spites
The sad and vulnerable who
Fed on sour delights
Acquire crude crafts,
Harangue and scowl
Leaving others to mother
And heal bleak language
Lethal cant
Has raped and sapped and fouled.

Abuse not words.

Abused they'll glow
Ephemerally then go
Blown with all who followed you.
Crippled language has no power
Blood may flow, true
But will not flower
Brothers. Momentary militants
Perhaps, whose words can dip
No deeper than their pocket's discontent.
The cheap linguistic cuts you take
Build no utopian avenues but soon unmake
Where once stood
Your lovely dreams of brotherhood.

Abuse not words.

All you found
Will be too easily brought down.
Words bruised rebound
Boomerang, flounder
Curse those who bruised them, stand
No longer than tomorrow's anger.

Would you weary energies
Burn out belief
Turn all you believed to disbelief
Affront your souls with bored liturgies?

What you fought lovingly to use
Do not abuse.
Abused words will explode
Revengefully when sent
For evidence and argument.
Those you harangue are not detained
Beyond intoxicated moment.

Be warned!
What is trifled with brings grief
Disappointment in old age.
The warm heart aches it aches
With cold ill-use
Shrill and chilled
Page after page after page.